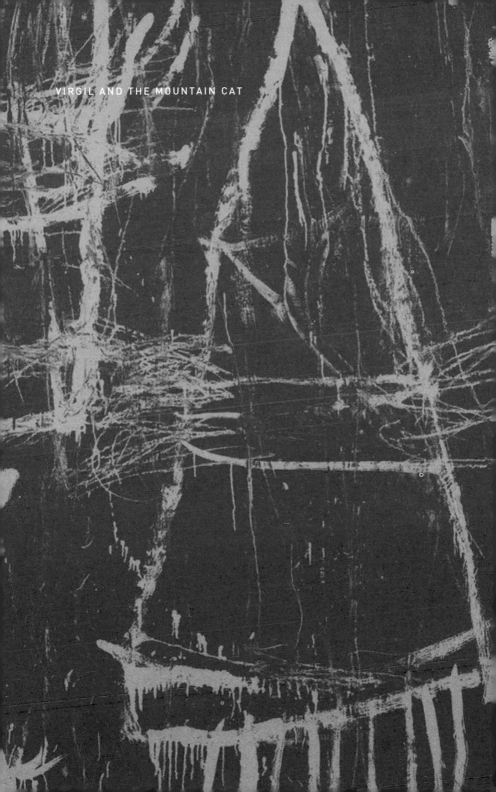

NEW CALIFORNIA POETRY

Edited by Robert Hass, Calvin Bedient, Brenda Hillman,
and Forrest Gander

VIRGIL AND THE MOUNTAIN CAT

POEMS

David Lau

UNIVERSITY OF CALIFORNIA PRESS   *Berkeley   Los Angeles   London*

University of California Press, one of the most distinguished university
presses in the United States, enriches lives around the world by advancing
scholarship in the humanities, social sciences, and natural sciences. Its
activities are supported by the UC Press Foundation and by philanthropic
contributions from individuals and institutions. For more information, visit
www.ucpress.edu.

University of California Press
Berkeley and Los Angeles, California

University of California Press, Ltd.
London, England

Library of Congress Cataloging-in-Publication Data

Lau, David, 1978–.
    Virgil and the mountain cat: poems / David Lau.
        p.   cm. — (New California poetry ; 25)
    Includes bibliographical references.
    ISBN 978-0-520-25873-0 (cloth : alk. paper)
    ISBN 978-0-520-25874-7 (pbk. : alk. paper)
    I. Title.
PS3612.A9425V57   2009
811'.6—dc22   2008021115

Manufactured in the United States of America

18   17   16   15   14   13   12   11   10   09
10   9   8   7   6   5   4   3   2   1

There's no such thing as life; or if there is,

It is faster than the weather, faster than
Any character. It is more than any scene:

Of the guillotine or of the glamorous hanging.

—Wallace Stevens, "Parochial Theme"

Yet Southern California at least by Lyellian
standards is a revolutionary, not a reformist
landscape. It is Walden Pond on LSD.

—Mike Davis, *Ecology of Fear*

CONTENTS

ACKNOWLEDGMENTS

Thanks to the editors of the publications in which some of the poems in this book first appeared (sometimes in slightly different forms):

The Bedazzler	"Apotheosis of Groundlessness"
	"Awkwardnesses"
	"Jellyfish"
	"Moved Only by Mechanical Device"
	"Oil Trees"
	"Parade"
	"Songs about the Avant-Garde"
	"Suburbatross"
Boston Review	"Boom Kiss Boom Boom Kiss"
Denver Quarterly	"Sir Not-Appearing-in-This-Film"
	"Songs about the Avant-Garde"
Fourteen Hills	"The Tupperware Concerto"
High Chair	"Extra Strength Resistant Resistance"
	"Protest in Philippines"
Jubilat	"Black Line Drawing"
	"Civil War"
New Orleans Review	"Vertigo Fastener"
Pool	"Immortality"
	"Tell Pearl"
Volt	"Day to Start on the Floorboards, Rain to the South, Any View a Machine"
	"Oil Trees"
	"Virgil and the Mountain Cat"
	"Yesterday Lectures"
Wildlife	"Yucca Flats"

Thanks to Alfred A. Knopf, a division of Random House, Inc., for permission to reprint an excerpt from Wallace Stevens's "Parochial Theme," and to Henry Holt and Company, LLC, for permission to reprint an excerpt from Mike Davis's *Ecology of Fear: Los Angeles and the Imagination of Disaster.*

This work was developed with criticism from many readers: Shane Book, Alexander Papanicolopoulos, Sandra Simonds, Chris Chen, Jon Thirkield, Claudia Rankine, Mark Levine, Jim Galvin, and Cole Swensen; enduring gratitude to Stephen Yenser; deepest thanks to my parents, Tom and Diane, and my brother, Matt. This book is dedicated to Maybelle McLaughlin: *I'm Nobody! Who are you?*

VIRGIL AND THE MOUNTAIN CAT

I

Prosopopoeia

Farewell drained fen—the judge, fielded
from a cautionary atmosphere's ruling body,
thinks a ship diagram clearly,

standing isolated in phlox reft of episode
only inches from. Unlabeled
Mundo tucked corner of rebozo under.
Keep moving. Keep the cough-ark's

collection dish moving. Horizon: that's where
what one wants to get down to needs material.
Body, one wants to get down.

Day to Start on the Floorboards, Rain to the South, Any View a Machine

Negative, chalk (how I first saw
your sign) reads like smoke signals.
Has an extensive collection of glasses.
On this side of the earth, no sides:
where we practice our marksmanship,
like soldiers in the city square, on corpses,
no matter many beetles in the grass.
Find it.
Obstinately refuse to grasp.
The spades, today valiantly shouldered,
submerge in the unprofitable patch.
Beetles are back-up plan zero,
the *if I were you* thing inside
the water container,
which is too blind to trust with the wheel,
to leave alone, even if in for the eve.
The wounds we gave ourselves
have just begun us,
irreligious, and are the deterrents,
as escarpments, of else but warlike heads.

Go get your own aquarium, each fin becoming
coiled beneath the bus, cruising along.
There you'll find the nasal passage.
Ask the operator for extreme commitment
from the lamp shade
to the table, all reflected in the unwashed window.

Table of omens. Flotation devices murmured
and murdered.
The shutters of thunder are forlorn
like the song of the sound of my own voice: a different
  tattooed country.
Nationalism.
At the rally, everybody's grin gives away two bags.
All are watered, her body slipping
out from under the dripping awning, effortlessly.

New Organic Shifts

You were a total honey
in the marked static's wild helmet,
pancake—all gleaming page of tools.
Text us the heatstroke you can see from space.
A mast of dice opens.
The Mallarmiste pens the proletarian novel:

The panda pattern dress
by the treed corazon
strike: snowed light
from the chemical plant
—the mottled map of condo leads
Athens-esque, its gusting razors for decks.
Fevered reef where—sudden beards—
root—an isn't—
you took me by Sears.

Suburbatross

Toward a gong between evergreens
pebbling shadows.

The coming apparition's contour in mustard
till morning. Way off

we frisked the amorous sea
the hooks broke down to hardness,

the unstoppable, tennis ball bottom
of my flamboyant peg table leg

which summons to bridges
certain vigils. Bigger,

a moist viceroy uncle-sorts the tunnel
entrance:

a blond, prone deschooling
lines still the fumigant blue.

Immortality

I lived alone.
I dwelt in stop signs
making cameos over.
Silver droned on
on the no-outlet bayswater
in a jejune drawl of box of holly
—but I was the tympanum in kerosene. Days
on the armed chaise bed from faux
SoHo (a figure eight in the catalogue
of prayers) also came along the never night
of malls in the dark.
(Beauty thing went bad to hearse.)
La belle femme skunk fatale
disappeared off the waning coast of whatever,
that other paradoxical self-negating reversal,
but what beautiful curves for a peanut grower
folktale. The zero sum song
of no one under 18, like a cagelessness, a tooth,
frayed from this gig's ongoingness.
At sunset I fetched a pail of snowmelt.

Meantime a thunderous oversoul cloud
of unknowing hankered after a public
keeping up a boatyard
and, oh,
to be me inside the annotations.
I was buried,

I lived alone, a spirit in a cellar
among the prescient vintage. Hyperbaton,
pseudoephedrine were once days
con pulpo ceviche and Proust's laptop.
Tennis was the hourglass. "Spirit is a bone,"
amalgam of signals,
photo-sculpture of her x-rayed.
None of it forged a hood for a head.
Go, on
the left-hand side the tufted former colony I nothing you starting out at.
Where the death moth of ours isn't proofed yet.

Going Out

You say nuclear; I say nuclear.
What kind of word is together?
On Cadmium dunes we treasure our Celts.
A plane to parachute from, a city: you want the radio:
if you want the radio for free charge the living: you have to,
ladies and dental plans. Sprig of mint
on the bib ineffective against further
spread of contagion.
In pain like a blouse,
this period is a peacock
in our history: drive the continent apart:
one lung left in the window
display of the BBQ restaurant.
City at the growth spurts of a city,
rubbing alcohol in the sun you say
and I say who else is in here? To leave the city,
to have to parachute into the middle of a crowd
in gowns, a hula hoop, into the hunt
for The Prussian State. At tail end,
fields of kelp:
pieces of the flight plan cover its thrush:
your interior tangle of wires. Sun's particulate jetsam
washes out the shore: runway cleared of caves
into which the cleanup crew is poured.
Your breath quits the ill-lit corridor.
All in the hangar, muchas prayers.

Man with Archiving Machine

They won't follow unless you pour concrete.
The chasms deep in red valley
—what could we help to destroy us?
The stomped hail knifed alone,
its palm like a sail farmed at sea: whitecap,
bellyroll. To counter the structural fragment

the manganese violet torch tore
invisible wake out, the light of these seas
captive of faraway days
like Myers, the clerk remotely from Yellow, while
unfocused—but brighter, now comelier stigma—
the post unfurthered a glide that half whistled,

in a shear zone of two movement-waters,
this oiled stuck-throughness
to leave the alphabets in shoe-ins.

Iovis Omnia Plena

You have a mug on your car, like a
nontraditional artist who questions? Word. Syllabic aperture.
The cloud shadow shore.
You say it is mini bears
automobilized the Saturday the people fled,
what the area saw was raw war.

Makeless. A scintillating strawberry picker
begins like Bolshevization's Chinese calligrapher
knotted mundo vagabundo across her glance's clasp,
the childlike phylum's tornadic atmospheres.

International Port of Los Angeles,
the belated reply to reality
deleted from art important in that situation
as apart are, belonged: limit on.

Happiness Is for the Terrestre

Dream home (title)
-lessness, chime-latmiya
where the linen machined foreign
-getfulness,—were they the
varied, useless Gargantua penta-gondola
array already (unemblematized ago) making
more perfect hat more stubborn
the houses come cloudlike harriers inside her
a great number streamlined into the adobe
to receive shock treatment forever.

A little metaphysical tsunami knocks us
viola elations. I don't think
I have as stars the peacock part of the center divider,
the bricks papering
a cell phone in tea.

My mouth formed around them (many),
the still style of steel on Grand.

Many Jasons

He strolled from the hill sound of sacred scales.
A sheet on his head (arrested for something),
they surrounded him,
Hera speaking through his mouth
kept the lid on his appeal to Caeneus the Lapith,
who had been a woman—
moon spread on the all edge of standing water,
the bleachers where they left the bodies.

That was the sedgy day, invisible contagions
stretching from our roof
on which the fresh trails of spilled pink . . .
to the aquatic plaza, one sandal at a time
and the bottom of the room beguiled us,
below the carpet covered with sand,
where they used to run
down the slums. Athena's oak prow, oracular,
from the grove at Dodona:
the team started the troika.

Many leave. One went in.
Many Jasons.
At some point Orpheus was on
that upside-down boat beneath the bridge,
but now, through its hull
(some planks missing), the ancestral bricks shimmer.
Rare is their tide.

Absolute, The

Well? Nothing.
Fig wasps make rapid detour
talk about thinking: He has partitioned
the grocer with priors.

Gut furnishings defanged the froideur
the lag summitted
in thrown space
plus force at fault don't change

a vivid square crisped by a quake gasp,
neutron star take away our
money in the trees
on the streets with the Marquise

feeds my mouth eye
lugging a dulcimer
at pure:
los drywalleros

many-motioned to Majorca.
Cries, a roar.
Stilled a pie,
mysterious takedown of a somber railing.

Tell Pearl

that amaranthine capitals dog us,
in Venezuela there's this bagatelle let's say,
and they crush a contested gust into guitars
in case of brushfires, wildfires, of intersections
carted away, so that there is no easy finger
in water, cup or sea, body or bay,
a marker to wrap ties around,
my ashlars as good as purple gold,
and into the act come reserves, come the TV wars.
So we went through the city with stops;
here into a gloaming with irregular bells,
into a bridge above, and, like a saturated
cliff's cascade here, into a chorus.

The Tupperware Concerto

The Tupperware concerto
    the domed 18th century   preenrolls in . . .
       it doesn't, it isn't   the same *none are*
of's alcoholic, Twomblyan   nightlong song-scape—
    we weakens us inside   another orchard,
     subject a predicate,   miscarvedly ancient
        violin, a cage,   courageous thassalocracy
      of its thrashings   in the garage

         could cause   widespread flooding.
     Kenyan sub-adult   qua chinoiserie's
   defunct spelunker of   a casino bungee jumper—
the happy '90s were sad.

      It was possible
    to beat the person soundly.

(The antique ode de me   is Walt Whitman's complete form.)

Black Line Drawing

Thug chandelier big time
and back down, man
with a dirty carrot in his mouth
at the bottom of some ladders that fabricate
watoosies. Platitude in the latitude
of the beatitudes. Shin.
FedEx-ualized ices tuba the poppy,
the post is kind. Please come. I love you very
much now. More than ever. I may die. You vary.

II

Oil Trees

Start in the snow.
Had to promise to endure.
Had to hold
the dome's cobalt exterior
beneath the faucet. Tearing heated water.
Had jettisoned the bucket.
Then on the snow, silhouette of two men,
a thrifty stretcher. Had already.

There were flashes of reservoir,
flashes nearly inflatable, and rosewood
for the cutthroat guitar.
The cold air stuck like leather to lungs.
Being in to reinvigorate the horde.
Stole the visage, levee of—
I poured
into the serving plate.

There were many
beneath these diamonds to climb on,
coding their arms, their knees.
From cilantro stalks
in the resistant sink,
go. A thousandth, near.

Awkwardnesses

The drums aren't sound this morning
in the elk-fog they have never been.

Accompanied the great grammar change, pipers
at the village of gates, and in the middle circle of each

were epoxy maps in the direction.
Blind woman I mulch,

why, why *our* Albany, Albany
black and white copied fenced Navy,

pitted and Nixoned as a peach into
a spiked retracting,

that smoke enclosed sorting of
the nickel libretti or

they'll wrap knuckles to radix for a limited time?

They Camped for This Day in the Villages Overlooking the Plain of the River

The more the malaria
crispness beyond torsion
bar of old Adidas, half an "o"
and a whole claps
from now on on me Oregon
storm coast livid with oil; a lawn liaising
verbatimized sunrise in lines of I-grade
reggae showcase.
                    Time jogged
or the bucketwash is bar code is
China's aborted Unocal takeover.

To solve whatever ailments in a lean
with a chisel when there was null
and these big city fire-hoop hippies,
like paleo-phratries
culled from counterrevolutionaries,
hit with that tweezed nipple lasso,
a curve so violent no line is tangent—
to bodies of incessant industry.

Sir Not-Appearing-in-This-Film

History is two blue jars traveling in opposite directions.
They will reach each other's one-man-gypsy-band tongue.
They will reach each other.
Tuft-bright grass crops up and down on us.
It's in the film about fisherman and excrement.

And a year passed
us postcards, trefoils, munched diadems,
with a silk of mud in its hair.
A cry from the cliff is only the smith.
I had stayed. I had to.

The sound is full of spruce needles.
They flange the shoal.
Above, below the house, the anfractuous path
leading down here is for dowers.
I am the inverse maid.

The Spy's Council of Breezes

Hurry up before our factory leaves.
The first column of the Freedom Tower
traduces its ensorcellment in the façade.
To take back the unit whole
disbarred of marble, the bound

beggar of church judiciality
in my tuxedo shirt. Solo passed
red rope networks, the world
drowns in her yawn, Persian gulf
dumber with the heliotropes.

At large with the happier New Year?
The way you treated me last year
there ain't nothing happy about it.
Back then the gas station's mini electric piano
invited to hebetude the tea root lion.

Civil War

I read, I write, I hate my life word after word.
Telescoping Mercury remains
a Septembrist in burglary,
eyebrows an overthrow

spring, snaky splinter
signal to another season, oppositional
turn back on the first day of the new?
The more mortal each jealous mischief/

All men are murderers the more the uneaten
fell out of charge as poems without words
(& i.e. etc./CSPN e.g. Enron
found in the anthology of aging aleatory broadsides),

our hundred-spoke limo wheels,
worked for two months in the Plaza Centre,
an Irvine Co. strip mall. Winded, changed,
sexual difference

made how we are San Diego
glow-bulge red snapper.
Pugnacious November.
Spieling a cackle for flute—asterisk—Iron

dawn
two weeks earlier. Awful
arcing calla spathe
most not alive, I wasn't afraid to die,

insensate, drugged, high
and the last Levi's plant barred its doors with oars
as the vegetarian told Pamela
he was taking good care of her lame horse.

Yucca Flats

Freedom reaches its notion in thought.
It leaves a bite mark on its ID photo

[rope tugs] [torso]

I live at once over it.
Satellite poker tourneys,
soju martinis,
and a flumpet chamois
amble by,

river of P-funk.

For the unsearch-termed
child with bolt action,
you were in the truckle

bed with the solar totals,
Im Dorfe, récit incomplet
de divers voyages.

In clover, you flopped
a feed bag phoenix
while I made oars with raised
lashes, unlimited calling

autographed by the rain
as surely the battlements
undergo cyst drainage
was how the movie ended,

reduced irritatingly.

In a gorge of whiplash
pigeons effect a great forgetting zone.

You were right before your original thought.

Stag

East of here, a lakelike spark,
so what type defense
the law firm tries depends on variable wind direction.
We give it to it. That dark.

The writing of the log
kept in the valley

of large qualities of lead
passed detonators
across the planted ferns
until the driver's verve was letterhead.

Metacinematic Skirt Border of a Traumatophile

Desperation? I couldn't remember.
To comb you with golf courses takes Visa
tae-kwon-doing her
handwriting at the festival of names I couldn't remember.
I waited the table of sanguine trains.
Spores about the foot of the bridge I was holding you out for.
Chlorine gas darkened Diyala,
Diwaniya sitting the constant car.

The end of your beautiful imprint:
seven white container cargo cranes
in one stretch of freeway.
We just hang out; the world works.

Parade

What are we going to tell our kids about
the sweet afternoon we went to the bazaar, Sunday?
At last, it seemed, day grasped
an oxygenated stare
as not recycling for recycling's sake.

I was trying to be free. I was contacted.
I went in shifts. I was onto love.
I was mandatory.
I was an access for the sun. I was last.
I went to my savings. I saved.

The crew is your nature signature. The hair is her.
Under the cleanup cylinder,
trainlike, category (airborne)
insists with a mammalian
filing cabinet seal.

Boom Kiss Boom Boom Kiss

She swore, pan soaping. I'm guessing brown bat, crow asunder le shawl-shaped collar. A needed house pith we sold gluttons. Her smell a discordant riddle, glyph of State bafflement. Sand lures all spines, heads, had drifters (bad) in charge not of ribbon that fell over her instep. She (bad) had naught self, a goner, biting paste, pen-shoulder, enveloped a thought. She had not herself to write to. She busted lure in kelp, booked her shelf, and in the mirror picked up a boy-look, as when, dreaming between the lines, there were moose on her geese. She belonged au travail or "No, go back!" to reaugment. He, daunted, a lie, but she chanted, "I'm a terrorist!"

Restlessness on the Hummock

1

They sleep together then they sleep.
Moisture in the recovery center
affects the combined torso of certain sinking wrecks.
Am I never
visiting the shepherds for lunch?

And couldn't you have turned the music down?
Occasional barn, the gray alternate
near the fretwork farmhouse, a bridge, the dutiful maturing
field, harvested or in a part.
Promptly the wedding's riposte, jumbo.

2

River the coyote noses you across. Moist coat—su hacha
binding the fledged hands, unless one of 'em

the bank in its fullness, nothing for cheap return
chalked on the board—am I never?

The moon roasts in its pit of games I play
like *are you older, Time,* and *bracelets.* Here is fear.

As we get further in I realize that you people
think things

funny I don't find funny at all.
That *x* is illiterate, the Huguenotic fever.

To an Ectopic Shepherd

Fever knocked us down from the hose
we were holding, down to Z-wear—
Who on the throw rug
kneels aside the king-size bed? Who wears copper
clouds to the track?

Hung on the approach
like gliders, we'd looped
plaid napkins around our ankles.
More and more we marry
in front of the window of the cleaning.

The squat guard screams, the fin in luggage.
He'd flipped through the roads.
Next morning we're head deep in profile.
We were, to the unstacked bucket.
Repairs to the record admit
tungsten and coal smoke.
This is the longest we've been led on for.

Apotheosis of Groundlessness

Stagnant air
unraveled every face

into infrequent station
wagons' bluesy refusal. The wall socket
whiff of hibiscus. Shivering.

No, let me go on my five-minute break
in the well-flung bell. Plead
with someone else's straw maw.

III

Tears Open the Sky behind Every Gesture

—mulberry
cargo on the darkness
charged train.

Milk mask,
horn headed,
we wore
the poor card.
A clerk
trifoliate swearing a country open.

There
went her murmurous boyhood
home, wasn't it, Ernie?

Where the arrow entered above and above.

Now Now There There You Know Her Skirt Settles on a Cow

Worship and wash up on sea
across falconry, forward.
The bones are the wealth of this mud.
Seeds, the bones we borrow. My arm going in
all over my head.
Sink in it my waking.

All's off with one shifted sleeve.
Bleach.
They go back and use.
They go back harder
than finding the fuse box here in the dark,
yet the house refurbished meadows.

Vertigo Fastener

You were burned
during beetle infestation as the other vagabonds and hooligans
crumbled bread

to each other were we calling to each other,
tones apart, tones in coincidental
sackcloth ions, sagging,

the calls welcoming
into the magazine an arc of a place inside stormed gates
of the never-seen: kept, pronounced.

Exclusion Act

Further the further I run.
You are where buffalo come from.
At the edge of thought is the carrier
of *an* explanation (indefinite, singular).

Round up the steeds, the daughters,
and the crystal ball they bought her.
I see a US Postal mailbox
or someone, back to me, arms crossed.

This land unfilled
with thistle
and short purplish threads, ashes,
vein, matches.

Scene

God stationed web out boasts rows.

Behold, in comes tax fan variable dirt summer.

Grape mask of wire rim glass of.

Nation bracelet case for a tire.

Open nerve at moth torso.

Bee broke in: news.

Candle Corporation of America.

Heroes of Our America

A dumped truck
of pigeons flocked to the carrefour; we couldn't continue on
with one flat fire. At home, trade
winds around the harbor, wheelchairs.
Previously I could see many faces

hammering the submerged chair deeper.
The next two, we said, are the last two
exits for the decentralized cargo.
Pining, in other words, for sound
of fewer things clockwise.

Night.
At the front door's threshold we jostled in our smudge
as though a last ray would come.
Gazing upon us, guests dropped off by gusts
failed to loosen their brutalism, bent fenders.

And the rest of the day while reciting
scraps for the harbor one wondered.
Had the chart been switched?
Water lilies confused with the drowned?
Meanwhile the store trickled into cars crossing

out—*in* the open, reserved motel.
Last night I copied out an unknown
character, unknown to me.
I'd written her of late. If she responds to the address,
its outcropping, where sand fills the net . . .

Domesticity Effect

Mirroraculous! blank and white, Jesuit Jacobin,
a domed frieze phrased in freedom,
extra moiety signum

as time's
dipterous nonextension
deemphasized dispatches to come—

incurable, its miserable son.
For their forgetting we have had make
poptastic psephologist plating setaceous in sage butter.

That's one? That's not bad. It was negative two this morning,
a shipwreck taking one of my supervisors
down, allegro misterioso.

I told her and one of my friends here at LACMA.
Pigeons landed on the lamppost above bus exhaust.
What is the ha ha part of the land,

à la exchange, did not age.

July Montaigne

The evacuation route
thudded loosely about her shoulders, a brochure
attached to Milton Friedman.

Correspondingly scorns for things holes
shoes sun dooms shares tolls
thunderclap shanghaied by the estuarial metropole,
drilled plate, starlit, leaded with blossoming carports—
the sea in ships—
The abs video ad business was my address once.
Me? The revolt of the eyes' Leather Plus,
a galactic ambush demonstration.

Toward Disunion's Opal

A fog direction
becomes louder,
becomes what we heard near the cindery splay
of a land dirty and burned and deedless,
a sea field (penumbra of pelicans),

orange thunder
limiting etcetera to the coming
anabasis.

Pounded out nest
in a brook abutting the cache,
its smuggled face
in the light end of hair—
cabinlessness
in the fused shallows.

Land Bridge

The acoustics of our yell surround
children in cattle costumes. *Cattle.*

Belts mark it
Pitch Mind, ferry me

over clothes arranged as crows
to a din of leaves.

Inside, flares light the rent:
wailers dyed their air red

before the universe. But the roots
came in relief

of washers, dryers on the one wires fence.
Straw in his hat of degrees.

"We graduated with him, this reflectedness."

Extra Strength Resistant Resistance

Fugue: torn clothes
man horizontal the oxcart
at the edged, mud-rocky field,
they tape parking lights
in the lippy defile

—to the shrapnel gardening goat child.
Revolt, the last gnomic moment,
stung clamor dirtier,
                            all helping,
people just having jobs,
instabstantial—martyrdom's fusion
of trysts—who had cars even?
Single, seeks weapons of mass destruction,
walks on the beach.
                            The wooziest jealousy
somehow committed
omnivorous in it: didn't
sex coruscatingly:
                            street
tongued in hospital
to inimical fruits
against her gazelle.

Songs about the Avant-Garde

1

in The Hague,
in the top down
hailstorm,
harp music clouding the hearing
of Webern
before he shattered in the head
leaving matins, a man, a one leg
minted
for Olympiad 1972,
counterrotations
of alarm clock arms
having not hands, songs
just before
the other guy
gets here, songs
in application of a warrant,
in unrecovered,
in waders and for Juárez
and further
stilts
engulfed,
song songs
in a ladle,
running their hands onto your faces
in the aetherlands, my lord,
in the convertible of their screams,
which didn't happen

until
he was
the only criminal, your flowing
skirt of nadir and lapel.

2

The reason I think
is because this is after.
(Branch berm composed to ankle shackles.)
What continues
keeps a corridor between string-playing peninsulas many months
later. The peninsula
after the peninsula where a tongue of stardust
going cold is spoken.
Woof. That's the nature of our field. Woof.
Ate all heart and gizzard. Woof. And rival fiber optics. Woof Woof.

                                Interference
is our category and we are wearing its
new line spring line from Milan and Cathay: Death of the Leaves.

A sudden
aquatint indicated a different period.
Call it après tennis.
Their equipment, an equipment
room, never would fit
in the Fountain Valley smorgasbord.

3

As an inhabitant, I continue
to live and think by grace
of an obsidian god. (Difference obtained.)
That's why dawns give such a fright.
That's why our frigate makes up ground
for interamnian people
in The Hague.
In the cave in The Hague
are wickedest lightenings,
stay put in the following.
In the cave with the painting and the monster in the painting with
   the cave.

Protest in Philippines

He is for a long time bleating the embassy collection:
(water-resistant cot,
a resurgent stretch of storefronts to dive into,
compadre, *con legno,* funding the new permits, pleasing
room, murderous rain.

Near-spring night, stars on flat blackboards, essay estate
questions passed person to person.
The lottery window
I turn red past,
hyacinth-lanced dawn.

In green tree talk
the transcriber dons a dark robe, a mirror.

The notebook discovered
the parting sun, magnificent trough, blind
hair on a head
of state, streak-woods
in the winding road atlas—stranded shore.

Pose in flight
covered by weeds, claw hair-rocks.
Pullulation. Push-up. Push-up.
Pestilentia reeds announce—trebly isolated, a closed trio,
the trinity trick-fucked—in a.

Where I Shall Need No Glass

The sign not in support of the cause
on the way to the way out really in a short, rank
jacket, the sign I realize.
The interior tariff
the man to me next says
switchboard knell for myrtle viburnum

　　　face of a scholar
　　　comes up with its eyes.

Get a dark keep down
(whole skull of the low school).
I had to leave in the existence of truth
where it wore a grove of resistance pilots
we thought were science fiction
neglected by its gear, the hammers just lying

　　　where we make our injured.

Moved Only by Mechanical Device

it's that their house-
's imbricate, forested fist burst

a double-paned
lagoon bottom

cash belching fit
in the space simulator

by Caspar David Friedrich
is an epic poem excluding history

Vietnam here
I was displaced stare

Feed, you ear

The Birth of Reality Out of Appearance

No depth to the sacred. No movement.
A barefoot hairdresser with a snare drum
up-armors the staunched,
the pro-Saddam (they were Mongoloids) before
payments on the debt dwarf
a liberating was, hurried, are the grooves?
'cause back then people could dance:
benevolent Wilsonianism and Wheat
Chex witnessed with Iraqis.

In a hotel, once, whole-hatchetly
you fuck-straightened Dawn
(Florida's aphasic, verdurous
vertigos and gradualisms goosey
like a go-cart). Who moved my groupuscule montage
militants in work's elementary unit: to clean up a stain?
Feel free to use the Danish bathing products.

"And then briefly I felt alive," said a kind of
Afrobeat ensemble notebook-ese koyo,
the unsuccessful mummy-leap
to postpone after by offering
ceaseless iterations of its absent
propagandist for the immemorial right,
a smarter version of everything.
Texas ice creams nothing resolved,

something forwarded: disorganization.
Better. Thailand is completely full of Thailand.
Out-creased the hooting lechuza, shack-strapped,
sunk under a stiff-upper-lip moon and
the social convention of immediate charity.

Seiche

A pig hinge, turf deodorant,
and the maze-freckle to build all the way up
to a car—abandoned
after one payment. Tools everywhere,

alive at ends.
And patients shifted their musk-weight around, a tree
rising on the oil-covered upholstery
with only one finger hole, an island

maneuver into canary cages
wanted

to save your sons,
wrapped to the rail; one end,

viscous rain.

The marching band in the marsh
fans out in the low wind, muddy wool to its knees.

Steam has a thousand wardrobes
and midday was to tousle cream blinds.
In here we're fitted with glasses, mint wrappers.
Peel off here.

Yesterday Lectures

Large lentils through the hole I give you.
Dear ms. grieving,
artificial turf in the rain gutters:
Anamnesis. Fifth-century Jutlands pinched just a little,
our probity at least, the paint flaked
on the worst part of the feeling:

                              out here a superconductor,
scores of bridal whores.
At eve bells bring out the blue.
Our knowledge, a phage with the napkin, the rainbow trout.
Sponsor or ponder us,
faded like bewilderment from the mare encounter.
The static is plastic to the touch.
Distrain my heart,
soft hatchet. Seal me over with coals.
Brushing your hair is the zipper's invention.
David? You must
believe if only to give up on the welcoming road, jonesing.

Virgil and the Mountain Cat

I was thinking I would like to own this house. Then I fell. Under hat, stone, cent, moss. Cranberry season into black smoke season. Plus a knife in the branchy flophouse.

She was coming at certain daytime, with interest. We were getting ready. Carried dishes that smelled like a hoax candle in the empty room. Nighttime followed the switch the guards used to guard everywhere it went on the mountain. As she, this changed. Cataracts went backward. The envelope stuck to licked dogwood. A day pianoed, swelled acutest, pianoed. Vanishing species to each other, plastic bags of grape leaves gave wind a concert on less tuned glass. Then.

Another overhead reverses the chorus. All is taken with her, taken away. Given the state, east in the union, crow parts way into the fence. Thoughts send out a little yellow cable, nothing to another town, and have. Been the letter writer with the three-part fishing pole.

The guards found her novel. I. Surgical instructions airlifted into the forest. II. Planes in "man missing" formation. III. Area dubbed a carpet for the procedure.

Knew. Knew alert. Those alarums her boy had bargained to us. The glow would lightbulb around his head as the sun banged down the western slope. The newspaper headline reported foreign container ships' rust flakes profuse in the harbor. So we were telling. It hadn't happened yet.

As the shore sounded.

Jellyfish

Dear XXth century
no one can darken skies like,

have you even been in meaning?

the forest on fire grows and glows
with sediment gorges hauled by

the clinking antiquated chain gaff:
words are worms more than what it's not:

"The Unnamable"   "The H Age"

a fucking sick hello, hymeneal subjoinder
from the whole fire and the sick

wick   halted   vertical   locks

by the riceless riverside

this who'll (if the smokes come)
carry the wind

you're hair in, there
being something you left.

"Immortality": The phrase "La belle femme skunk fatale" is from the animated cartoon *For Scenti-mental Reasons,* directed by Chuck Jones. The phrase "Spirit is a bone" is from G. W. F. Hegel's *Phenomenology of Spirit,* translated by A. V. Miller (Oxford: Oxford University Press, 1977).

"Iovis Omnia Plena": The title (which translates as "Jove, all powerful") is from "Eclogue III" of Virgil's *The Eclogues.*

"Many Jasons": The title is from William Shakespeare's *The Merchant of Venice.*

"They Camped for This Day in the Villages Overlooking the Plain of the River": The title is from Xenophon's *Anabasis,* translated by Rex Warner (as *The Persian Expedition* [London: Penguin, 1975]).

"Sir Not-Appearing-in-This-Film": The title is from the film *Monty Python and the Holy Grail,* directed by Terry Gilliam and Terry Jones.

"The Spy's Council of Breezes": My heliotropes for Arthur Rimbaud's "Oraison du soir" and "Chant de guerre parisien." For a relevant discussion, see Kristin Ross, *The Emergence of Social Space: Rimbaud and the Paris Commune* (Minneapolis: University of Minnesota Press, 1988).

"Civil War": "All men are murderers" is an aphorism from Wallace Stevens's *Adagia* (in *Wallace Stevens: Collected Poetry and Prose* [New York: Library of America, 1997]).

"Yucca Flats": The title is a truncation of the film title *The Beast of Yucca Flats* (directed by Coleman Francis). "Im Dorfe" is the seventeenth song in Franz Schubert's song cycle *Winterreise,* a setting of a sequence of poems by Wilhelm Müller. "Récit incomplet de divers voyages" is the subtitle of Michael Haneke's film *Code inconnu.*

"Tears Open the Sky behind Every Gesture": The title is from Walter Benjamin's *Illuminations,* translated by Harry Zohn (New York: Schocken Books, 1968).

"Protest in Philippines": The phrase *con legno* denotes the violin technique of using the wood of the bow on the string(s).

"Moved Only by Mechanical Device": The title is Ezra Pound's note to his translation of Guido Cavalcanti's sonnet "Tu m'hai sì piena di dolor la mente," in *Ezra Pound: Translations* (New York: New Directions, 1963). The phrase "Vietnam here" is the Los Angeles Police Department's characterization of its 1980s anti-gang sweeps (see Mike Davis, "The Hammer and the Rock," in his *City of Quartz: Excavating the Future in Los Angeles* [New York: Verso, 1990]).